EXPLORE THE UNITED STATES

IDAHO

Sarah Tieck

Big Buddy Books

An Imprint of Abdo Publishing
abdobooks.com

abdobooks.com

Published by Abdo Publishing, a division of ABDO, PO Box 398166, Minneapolis, Minnesota 55439.
Copyright © 2020 by Abdo Consulting Group, Inc. International copyrights reserved in all countries.
No part of this book may be reproduced in any form without written permission from the publisher.
Big Buddy Books™ is a trademark and logo of Abdo Publishing.

Printed in the United States of America, North Mankato, Minnesota
102019
012020

THIS BOOK CONTAINS
RECYCLED MATERIALS

Design: Aruna Rangarajan, Mighty Media, Inc.
Production: Mighty Media, Inc.
Editor: Liz Salzmann

Cover Photograph: Shutterstock Images
Interior Photographs: AP Images, pp. 21, 23; Charlie Litchfield/AP Images, p. 9 (bottom left);
    HAROLD VALENTINE/AP Images, pp. 22, 27 (top right); Isaac Brekken/AP Images, pp. 18 (inset),
    29 (top left); Shutterstock Images, pp. 4, 5, 6, 7, 9, 10, 11, 13, 14, 15, 16, 17, 20, 24, 25, 26, 27,
    28, 29, 30; TomFullum/iStockphoto, pp. 18, 19

Populations figures from census.gov

Library of Congress Control Number: 2019943179

Publisher's Cataloging-in-Publication Data
Names: Tieck, Sarah, author.
Title: Idaho / by Sarah Tieck
Description: Minneapolis, Minnesota : Abdo Publishing, 2020 | Series: Explore the United States |
    Includes online resources and index.
Identifiers: ISBN 9781532191152 (lib. bdg.) | ISBN 9781532177880 (ebook)
Subjects: LCSH: U.S. states--Juvenile literature. | Western States (U.S.)--Juvenile literature. | Physical
    geography--United States--Juvenile literature. | Idaho--History--Juvenile literature.
Classification: DDC 979.6--dc23

CONTENTS

ONE NATION

The United States is a diverse country. It has farmland, cities, coasts, and mountains. Its people come from many different backgrounds. And, its history covers more than 200 years.

Today the country includes 50 states. Idaho is one of these states. Let's learn more about Idaho and its story!

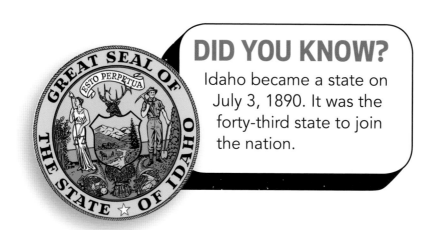

DID YOU KNOW?

Idaho became a state on July 3, 1890. It was the forty-third state to join the nation.

Idaho is known for its natural beauty. The Snake River (*pictured*) and the Rocky Mountains run through the state.

CHAPTER 2

IDAHO UP CLOSE

The United States has four main regions. Idaho is in the West.

Idaho has six states on its borders. Nevada and Utah are south. Washington and Oregon are west. Montana and Wyoming are east. And, the country of Canada is north.

Idaho has a total area of 83,569 square miles (216,443 sq km). About 1.7 million people live in the state.

Puerto Rico became a US commonwealth in 1952.

DID YOU KNOW?

Washington, DC, is the US capital city. Puerto Rico is a US commonwealth. This means it is governed by its own people.

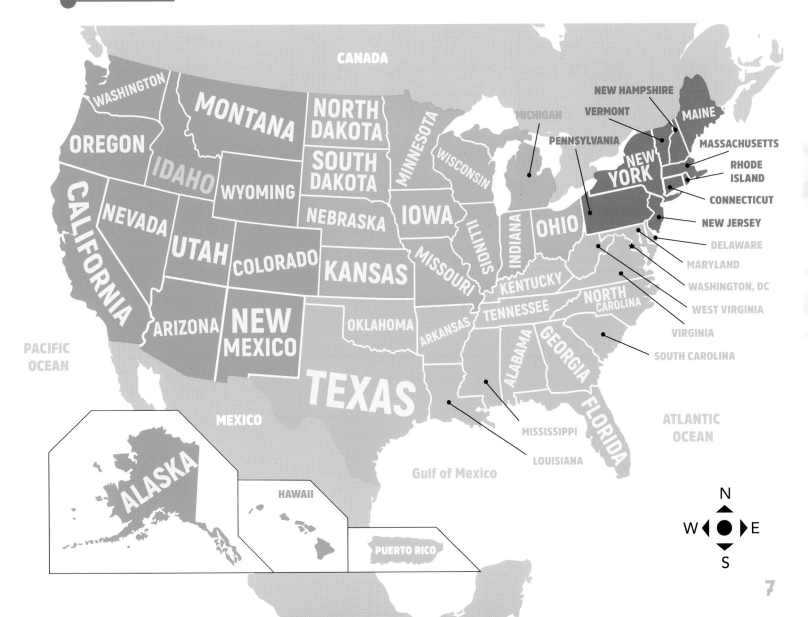

Regions of the United States

West
Midwest
South
Northeast

CANADA

WASHINGTON
OREGON
MONTANA
NORTH DAKOTA
SOUTH DAKOTA
IDAHO
WYOMING
CALIFORNIA
NEVADA
UTAH
COLORADO
NEBRASKA
IOWA
ARIZONA
NEW MEXICO
KANSAS
OKLAHOMA
TEXAS

MINNESOTA
WISCONSIN
MICHIGAN
ILLINOIS
INDIANA
OHIO
MISSOURI
KENTUCKY
TENNESSEE
ARKANSAS
MISSISSIPPI
ALABAMA
GEORGIA
LOUISIANA
FLORIDA
NORTH CAROLINA
SOUTH CAROLINA

NEW HAMPSHIRE
VERMONT
MAINE
PENNSYLVANIA
NEW YORK
MASSACHUSETTS
RHODE ISLAND
CONNECTICUT
NEW JERSEY
DELAWARE
MARYLAND
WASHINGTON, DC
WEST VIRGINIA
VIRGINIA

PACIFIC OCEAN

MEXICO

ATLANTIC OCEAN

ALASKA

HAWAII

PUERTO RICO

Gulf of Mexico

N
W E
S

7

CHAPTER 3

IMPORTANT CITIES

Boise (BOY-see) is Idaho's state capital and largest city. It is home to 228,790 people.

Boise is on the Boise River. When French fur trappers arrived in the 1800s, the river was lined with trees. So, Boise got its name from *boisé*, which is French for "wooded." Today, Boise is sometimes called the "City of Trees."

MERIDIAN is known for the Village at Meridian, which has shops, restaurants, theaters, and a show fountain.

BOISE has been Idaho's capital since 1864. The capitol building can be seen above many other buildings in the city.

NAMPA The Snake River Stampede is a rodeo held every July in Nampa.

Boise's parks have trees from around the world. US presidents and other leaders have brought the trees as gifts.

Meridian is the state's second-largest city. It is home to 106,804 people. Its population grew by nearly 150 percent between 2000 and 2015!

Nampa is the third-largest city in Idaho. Its population is 96,252. It is located near the Snake River. Nampa was founded in 1886 on a railroad line.

CHAPTER 4

IDAHO IN HISTORY

Idaho's history includes Native Americans, explorers, and gold. Native Americans have lived in present-day Idaho for thousands of years. Many lived near rivers and fished for salmon. Others moved around, hunting buffalo.

In 1805, Meriwether Lewis and William Clark explored the area. Then in 1860, gold was found. This brought many people to the land. Idaho became a US territory in 1863. It became a state in 1890.

DID YOU KNOW?

Before settlers arrived, many Native American tribes lived in Idaho. The Shoshone (shuh-SHOHN) and Nez Percé (NEHZ-PUHRS) were among the main tribes.

Lewis and Clark were American explorers. They traveled across the United States from 1804 to 1806.

CHAPTER 5

ACROSS THE LAND

Idaho has mountains, valleys, and canyons. The Rocky Mountains, or Rockies, cover most of Idaho. The Rockies are North America's longest mountain chain! The Snake River also flows through the state.

Many types of animals live in Idaho. These include trout, grouse, and deer. There are even gray wolves and grizzly bears in small numbers.

DID YOU KNOW?

Idaho's average high temperature in July is 87°F (31°C). In January, it is 34°F (1°C).

The Snake River is Idaho's longest river. It has powerful dams that provide electricity for the state.

CHAPTER 6

EARNING A LIVING

Farming, manufacturing, and mining are important businesses in Idaho. Farmers grow potatoes, wheat, and beets. Factories make computer parts and food products. And, silver and sand are mined in Idaho.

In recent years, Idaho has become a popular vacation spot. So, many people have jobs helping visitors.

DID YOU KNOW?
Idaho grows one-third of the potatoes in the United States.

Many people visit Sun Valley for ski vacations.

CHAPTER 7

SPORTS PAGE

Many people think of outdoor sports when they think of Idaho. People like to hunt, fish, golf, and ski there.

College sports are also popular in Idaho. Boise State University has a strong football team. The University of Idaho and Idaho State University also have popular sports teams.

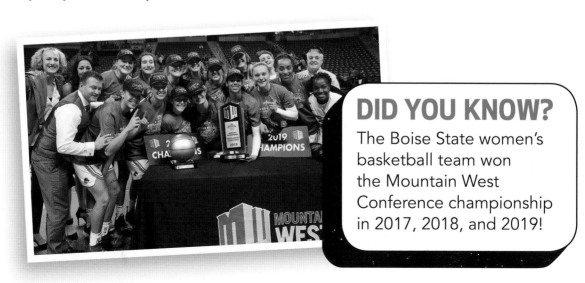

DID YOU KNOW?

The Boise State women's basketball team won the Mountain West Conference championship in 2017, 2018, and 2019!

The Lochsa River is a popular Rocky Mountain rafting spot.

CHAPTER 8

HOMETOWN HEROES

Many famous people are from Idaho. Gutzon Borglum was born near Bear Lake in 1867. He was a sculptor.

Borglum is known for creating the sculpture on Mount Rushmore in South Dakota. He began work carving the faces of four American presidents there in 1927. Borglum worked on the project until he died in 1941. His son finished it.

DID YOU KNOW?

Mount Rushmore includes the faces of George Washington, Thomas Jefferson, Theodore Roosevelt, and Abraham Lincoln (*left to right*).

Carving Mount Rushmore was dangerous work! Borglum (*far left*) directed workers high above the valley.

Several famous athletes are from Idaho. Baseball great Harmon Killebrew was born in Payette in 1936. He became part of the National Baseball Hall of Fame in 1984.

Downhill skier Picabo Street was born in Triumph in 1971. She raced in the Winter Olympics in 1994, 1998, and 2002.

DID YOU KNOW?
Killebrew played with the Minnesota Twins for most of his career.

Street won an
Olympic gold
medal in 1998!

CHAPTER 9

A GREAT STATE

The story of Idaho is important to the United States. The people and places that make up this state offer something special to the country. Together with all the states, Idaho helps make the United States great.

The highest point in Idaho is Borah Peak. It is 12,662 feet (3,859 m) high!

Shoshone Falls is on the Snake River. The falls drop down 212 feet (65 m)!

TIMELINE

1860

A gold rush began after gold was found in Orofino Creek. Over the next few years, many people came to the area in search of gold.

1890

Idaho became the forty-third state on July 3.

1800s

1900s

Lewis and Clark explored Idaho.

1805

Boise became the **capital** of the Idaho Territory.

1864

The first Spud Day was held in Shelley. This yearly festival was named for potatoes, one of Idaho's major products.

1927

1959

The Snake River's Brownlee Dam was completed. It is the largest dam in the Hells **Canyon** area.

2011

Harmon Killebrew died on May 17. He was buried in Riverside Cemetery in Payette.

2018

Idaho's population grew more than 35 percent between 2000 and 2018. The average US population growth was about 16 percent.

2000s

Idaho celebrated 100 years as a state.

1990

The Village at Meridian opened in Meridian.

2013

TOUR BOOK

Do you want to go to Idaho? If you visit the state, here are some places to go and things to do!

TASTE
Idaho is famous for growing Russet Burbank potatoes. Try one baked, fried, or mashed!

LOOK
Many animals live in Idaho. You might see elk, bighorn sheep, mountain goats, wolves, and even bears!

Idaho is one of only a few states where sage grouse live.

CHEER

Catch a Boise State University football game at Albertsons Stadium. It is known for its blue turf!

The stadium has had blue turf since 1986.

DISCOVER

Hells Canyon is the deepest canyon in the United States. Its deepest spot drops down 7,900 feet (2,400 m)!

LEARN

Visit Craters of the Moon National Monument and Preserve. It is known for its unusual rock shapes and cracked land.

FAST FACTS

▶ STATE FLOWER
Syringa

▶ STATE TREE
Western
White Pine

▶ STATE BIRD
Mountain Bluebird

▶ STATE FLAG:

▶ NICKNAME:
Gem State

▶ DATE OF STATEHOOD:
July 3, 1890

▶ POPULATION (RANK):
1,754,208
(39th most-populated state)

▶ TOTAL AREA (RANK):
83,569 square miles
(14th largest state)

▶ STATE CAPITAL: Boise

▶ POSTAL ABBREVIATION:
ID

▶ MOTTO:
"Esto Perpetua"
(Let It Be Perpetual)

GLOSSARY

athlete—a person who is trained or skilled in sports.

canyon—a long, narrow valley between two cliffs.

capital—a city where government leaders meet.

diverse—made up of things that are different from each other.

region—a large part of a country that is different from other parts.

sculptor—an artist who carves stone, wood, metal, or something else to form art. A sculpture is the art formed by one of these artists.

ONLINE RESOURCES

Booklinks
NONFICTION NETWORK
FREE! ONLINE NONFICTION RESOURCES

To learn more about Idaho, please visit **abdobooklinks.com** or scan this QR code. These links are routinely monitored and updated to provide the most current information available.

INDEX